123 SESAME STREET®

D0382230

Watch Out for Banana Peels

and Other Important Sesame Safety Tips

By Sarah Albee
Illustrated by Tom Brannon

"Sesame Workshop"®, "Sesame Street"®, and associated characters, trademarks, and design elements are owned and licensed by Sesame Workshop. ©2000, 2010 Sesame Workshop. All Rights Reserved.

Published by Creative Edge, 2010, an imprint of Dalmatian Publishing Group, Franklin, Tennessee 37067. No part of this book may be reproduced or copied in any form without written permission from the copyright owner. 1-800-815-8696

Printed in China

CE12916/0410/ZHE

Hello there, boys and girls! I am Officer Grover, and this is my Safety Deputy, Elmo. We have some very important safety tips to tell you about today. Here is the first one!
SAFETY TIP #1:
Be careful turning the pages of a book so you don't get a paper cut.

SAFETY TIP #3: Always wear a helmet and safety gear when riding a bike or skating.

SAFETY TIP #4: Never pet a strange dog.

That is all we have time for today. Congratulations! Now you can be a Safety Deputy, too Here is a badge. Ask a grownup to help you trace it, cut it out, and stick it on.
WAIT! Deputy Elmo has one last safety tip. Do not leave your safety badge lying around where someone might sit on it.
SAFETY DEPUTY
SP